MIDLOTHIAN PUBLIC LIBRARY

3 1614 00196 1

W9-BHU-325

ANTIMATTER
EXPLAINED

JUV
5231
GAU

THE MYSTERIES OF SPACE

ANTIMATTER EXPLAINED

RICHARD GAUGHAN

MIDLOTHIAN PUBLIC LIBRARY
14701 S. KENTON AVENUE
MIDLOTHIAN, IL 60445

Enslow Publishing
101 W. 23rd Street
Suite 240
New York, NY 10011
USA
enslow.com

JUV
523.1
GAU

For Rachel. If only there were anti-cats…

Acknowledgements

Thanks to the staff at the Cline Library for
helping ensure access to quality information.

Published in 2019 by Enslow Publishing, LLC.
101 W. 23rd Street, Suite 240, New York, NY 10011

Copyright © 2019 by Enslow Publishing, LLC

All rights reserved.

No part of this book may be reproduced by any means without the written permission of the
publisher.

Library of Congress Cataloging-in-Publication Data

Names: Gaughan, Richard, author.
Title: Antimatter explained / Richard Gaughan.
Description: New York : Enslow Publishing, [2019] | Series: The mysteries of
space | Audience: Grades 7 to 12. | Includes bibliographical references
and index.
Identifiers: LCCN 2018012871| ISBN 9781978504530 (library bound) | ISBN
9781978505544 (pbk.)
Subjects: LCSH: Antimatter—Juvenile literature. |
Matter—Properties—Juvenile literature. | Cosmology—Juvenile literature.
Classification: LCC QC173.36 .G385 2018 | DDC 530.4—dc23
LC record available at https://lccn.loc.gov/2018012871

Printed in the United States of America

To Our Readers: We have done our best to make sure all websites in this book were active and
appropriate when we went to press. However, the author and the publisher have no control over
and assume no liability for the material available on those websites or on any websites they
may link to. Any comments or suggestions can be sent by email to customerservice@enslow.
com.

Photos Credits: Cover, pp. 8–9 GiroScience/Shutterstock.com; p. 5 d1sk/Shutterstock.com;
p. 7 vchal/Shutterstock.com; p. 14 Cordelia Molloy/Science Source; p. 16 Science History
Images/Alamy Stock Photo; p. 18 Print Collector/Hulton Fine Art Collection/Getty Images; p. 22
chromatos/Shutterstock.com; p. 25 Science & Society Picture Library/Getty Images; pp. 26, 39
Encyclopaedia Britannica/Universal Images Group/Getty Images; p. 28 general-fmv
/Shutterstock.com; p. 29 snapgalleria/Shutterstock.com; p. 32 yaruna/Shutterstock.com;
pp. 36–37 Kenneth Eward/BioGrafx/Science Source/Getty Images; p. 40, 46, 50–51 Bettmann
/Getty Images; p. 44 Fouad A. Saad/Shutterstock.com; p. 49 BanksPhotos/E+/Getty Images;
p. 57 Lionel Flusin/Gamma-Rapho/Getty Images; pp. 59, 60 Designua/Shutterstock.com; p. 61
chromatos/Shutterstock.com; p. 66 Andrea Danti/Shutterstock.com; p. 68 Chronicle
/Alamy Stock Photo; back cover and interior pages sdecoret/Shutterstock.com (earth's
atmosphere from space), clearviewstock/Shutterstock.com (space and stars).

CONTENTS

INTRODUCTION

The aliens are closing in; the weapons systems are out. Captain Kirk calls down to the engine room, "Scotty, get me more power!"

"I can't, Captain; the matter-antimatter containment is already pushed to its limit. If we drive any harder, it'll blow!"

The aliens are imaginary. The ship is imaginary. Even Captain Kirk and Scotty are imaginary. But antimatter is real. And if enough matter and antimatter were to collide, the result *would* be a gigantic explosion.

Just as the word says, antimatter is "*anti*-matter." That is, it's the opposite of matter. It's hard, though, to imagine the opposite of, for example, a gray rock. Perhaps the "anti-gray rock" would be something like a green stalk of celery or a pile of pink cotton candy. But if a rock mashed a stalk of celery there would be a puddle of celery juice, not a giant explosion. And the pink cotton candy might make a sticky rock, but still no explosion. So antimatter must be something different than any specific "anti" object one can think of.

To understand antimatter, first one has to understand matter. If a rock is split in half, the result is two smaller rocks. If one of those half-rocks is split, then the result is two half half-rocks. The rock can be split and split over and over again, and the result will still be a mound of tiny rocks.

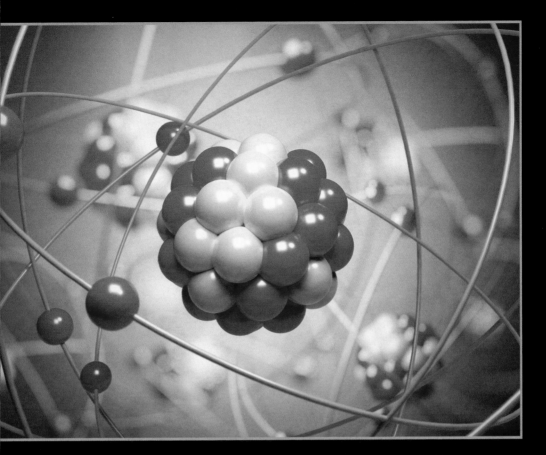

For many years, atoms were thought to be the smallest possible bits of matter. Then experiments revealed that atoms themselves are composed of tiny electrons whirling around a center—a nucleus—composed of heavier protons and neutrons.

There is a time, though, when the tiny rocks can't be split any further. In fact, those tiny bits of matter aren't even rocks anymore. Those bits are atoms, and for many years, scientists thought atoms were the tiniest possible bits of matter.

Our universe is built from matter, such as electrons, protons, and neutrons. But for every particle there is an antiparticle. When a particle and its antiparticle meet, the result is total annihilation and the release of energy.

It turns out, however, that atoms can also be split into even tinier bits. And some of those even tinier bits can also be split into bits that are even smaller. Those tiny particles go by names such as electrons, protons, and neutrons. A group of other particles called quarks are named bottom, top, charm, strange up, and down. But all those bits are composed of matter.

Things get even stranger: most of those tiny particles have antiparticles. Unlike an "anti-rock," these antiparticles are exact duplicates, except that, in some sense that scientists don't completely understand, they are not quite duplicates, they are exact opposites. They have the same weight, but are opposite in every other way. They are such exact opposites that they will completely destroy one another when they make contact with each other.

That brings up another important question: if all these tiny particles have antiparticles, why aren't particles and antiparticles crashing into each other all around us? If that were happening, it wouldn't be a secret, because every crash would make an explosion.

That remains one of the mysteries of the universe. Scientists know of no reason that there should be more electrons than antielectrons (called positrons), and no reason there should be more protons than antiprotons. The universe, as far as scientists can tell, is made up of matter and not antimatter.

Just because there's not much antimatter around doesn't mean scientists can't study it. Scientists can make antimatter particles, and they have even built antimatter atoms. They build these particles in huge machines called particle accelerators, and the measurements they make may lead to answers about the material that makes up the universe.

The road to an understanding of antimatter begins with an understanding of matter. That quest begins with a question people have been asking for thousands of years: what is the universe made of?

Chapter One

Asking the Right Questions

It's easy to think ancient people were stupid. There are so many things they didn't know:

- The brain is used for thinking.
- Earth travels around the sun.
- Living organisms usually reproduce by combining genetic material from two parents.
- Many diseases are due to infection from microscopic organisms, germs.
- All matter is built from one set of about 120 different atoms.

But not knowing something—ignorance—is different from being smart—intelligence. To learn anything, humans need to have a question and try to get an answer. To get the answers, they needed to be smart. Early humans had questions such as:

- Will I die if I eat this?
- How do I hit two rocks together to make a sharp tool?
- How can I keep that lion from eating me?
- How can I make a fire to keep warm?

After they answered those questions (and passed the answers down to their children), they asked new questions:

- When should we plant seeds to make sure we have enough food to survive?
- How can we work together to protect each other and make sure everyone has enough to eat?
- How can we make shelters?

Then came new questions. It's important to notice that they could ask new questions only because they already had the answers to the earlier questions. They knew how to keep safe from lions, when to plant crops, how to stay cozy in buildings, and how to live close enough to each other to be able to cooperate on all those tasks. That is, they knew how to stay alive. They weren't smarter than their ancestors, but they were less ignorant.

Now that they had those answers, they could ask a question that is still interesting: what makes up everything in the world?

Searching for Answers

Imagine you are ignorant about anything to do with matter. All you know is that there are two parts of the world. The first part is what's happening inside you—you're hungry, you're sad, or you're tired. The second part is everything outside of you. This external world has air to breathe, water to drink, rocks with which to build, and fire with which to cook. Now the question is: what makes up all these things in the external world?

The simplest explanation is that each kind of object is made up of exactly what it appears to be. Rock is built from rock. Wood is built from wood. Air is air. But ancient humans' observations made them think there must be a deeper reality, one they *couldn't* easily see. They thought about the question. They didn't need to figure out how to survive, so they could think about things that weren't directly related to finding enough food or protecting themselves from the weather or other dangers. That kind of thinking is called philosophy.

Look at a fire. A solid object, such as a piece of wood, heats up and turns into fire. But the fire itself eventually disappears. It turns into air. How would you explain that? You see a solid turn into fire turn into air. If that can happen, it makes sense to think that it can work backward, too. Air can turn into fire and fire can turn into a solid object.

A few thousand years ago, the ancient Greeks came to that exact conclusion.[1] Perhaps they weren't the first people to think about what makes up the world, but they were the first to write it down, so they get the credit.

But the ancient Greeks didn't all have the same explanation for the nature of matter. Some, such as Thales of Miletus (624–546 BCE), reportedly thought that everything was created from water, squished and pressed into different forms. Anaximander (c. 610–c. 546 BCE) thought there was an invisible substance called *apeiron*. All other things, he thought, were created from apeiron. Another Greek philosopher, Empedocles (492–432 BCE), thought there had to be more than one type of substance; he thought everything was a mix of air, fire, water, and earth.[2] Some of these ancient thinkers even thought that matter was composed of tiny invisible pieces called atoms. These atoms, of different shapes, could clump together in different ways to make all the material in the world.[3]

The philosophers who thought about these questions got their ideas from looking at the world, from making observations.

More than two thousand years ago, the Greek philosopher Democritus created a mental model of the universe with Earth and the planets in the center, the stars surrounding them, and an outermost region he described as "infinite chaos." Part of his idea was that matter was composed of tiny, unbreakable specks he called atoms.

But to them, thought was just as important as their observations. They had never seen water turn into a rock, but because the idea made some sense to them, they could convince themselves it was probably true. It wasn't until more than a thousand years later that an Arab scientist named Abu Ali al-Hasan Ibn al-Haytham (965–1040 CE) figured out that testing was more important than thinking. Or at least *as* important.[4]

CURIOUS ABOUT THE WORLD

No one really knows how early humans learned the value of fire, or how they realized that planting crops would increase available food. But one thing is certain: they wouldn't have come up with those answers if they weren't asking the right questions. That's pretty good evidence that curiosity has been part of human nature as long as there have been humans.

Curiosity lies at the heart of all science, because scientists are all trying to do one thing: answer a question to which no one else knows the answer. Scientists try to fit their answers into a model of the world. Around the year 1900, their answers weren't fitting, so they needed to find a new model. Antimatter would be an important part of that new model.

Abu Ali al-Hasan Ibn al-Haytham was the first person to say that observations and experiment were more important than just thinking. That is, no matter how much an idea makes sense, said al-Haytham, if the observations don't match the idea, that means something about the idea is wrong. This image shows what later artists thought al-Haytham might have looked like, as no drawings were made of him when he was alive.

There was no internet in the year 1000, when al-Haytham did his work. In fact, even the printing press had not yet been invented—every book needed to be copied out by hand. So it took hundreds of years for al-Haytham's ideas to spread. It took a few hundred more years before technology got good enough to make some more tests about the nature of matter. But when the technology was ready, scientists were ready to investigate.

Testing the Nature of Matter

Before the middle of the 1800s, people studying the physical world were called natural philosophers. They were studying the "natural" world, as opposed to the "created" world of ideas, laws, money, and art. But they were still philosophers. That is, they did a lot of thinking about how things should be. It seems logical, for example, that heavy objects would fall faster than light objects, so they figured that must be true. In reality, though, careful observations by Galileo Galilei (1564–1642) and Robert Boyle (1627–1691) showed that heavy and light objects fall at exactly the same rate, unless some other influence, such as wind or air resistance, affects them differently.[5]

As the ideas of al-Haytham and others were spreading, these natural philosophers were basing more of their thinking on direct observations. They were giving less weight to the way things *should* be, and more weight to the way things *are*. The people doing this new kind of study deserved a new name, and in the middle of the 1800s, British philosopher William Whewell (1794–1866) came up with that new name: scientist.[6]

These people were no longer called philosophers, but they still needed to think; they just thought in a different way. Scientists make observations and do experiments, and they try to fit their observations into a mental model of the world.

In the sixteenth century, Galileo Galilei experimented with dropping heavy and light objects at the same time. His observations showed a new idea must be correct: objects fall at the same speed, no matter how heavy they are.

Those mental models are called theories. Sometimes scientists making observations and doing experiments come up with new information that changes the mental model, the theory. Sometimes scientists working on the theory end up ahead of the people making experiments. Putting that another way: sometimes a measurement is completely unexpected, and other times, a surprising measurement is predicted before it is ever observed.

Both things have happened in the history of antimatter. But the first steps in the science of matter were pushed along by observations and experiments—and the return to one of the ideas of the ancient Greeks.

Chapter Two

Finding the Atom

Imagine standing inside a bakery looking at a shelf full of baked goods. They all look the same, round with a flaky brown top. Unfortunately, the baker has gone home without labelling the tasty things on the shelf, and the person behind the counter just started working there today. He has no idea what's what.

How are you going to figure out what's for sale? The bakery worker will have to slice into each of the items. What if the only tool around was a hammer? The clerk could bring the hammer down on each one of the items and break them into pieces. The shattered remnants would show what was in each baked good. It would be messy, and the baker wouldn't be very happy that her inventory was splattered all over the shop, but at least the answer to the mystery would be revealed: you would know which items were scones, which were bread, which were apple pies, and which were berry pies.

But if the bakery offers blueberry, huckleberry, and blackberry pies, there's trouble, because they all look the same. But the clerk still has the hammer, so he can find a clump of dark bluish pie filling and give it another smash. Looking at the smaller pieces will show whether it has the tiny soft seeds of the blueberry, medium-sized harder seeds of the huckleberry, or big hard seeds of the blackberry.

The ingredients were revealed when the bakery clerk put energy into the pies to break them into smaller pieces then looked at those smaller pieces. That's essentially what scientists do when they want to determine what makes up a material.

Chemists Get to Work

By the late 1800s, chemists had discovered some ways to split up materials and examine them. Sometimes they would grind up a material, sometimes heat it up, and sometimes expose the material to another chemical, such as an acid. All those are ways of putting energy into a material to split it up. Using those methods, chemists figured out that there were two different types of materials. Some materials, such as copper and oxygen, can be broken into smaller and smaller pieces and still stay the same. That is, the tiniest bit of copper acts just like a big piece of copper that was shrunk down—it takes part in the same chemical reactions. They called those materials *elements*. They named the smallest bits of the elements *atoms*—based on the word invented by the ancient Greeks.

Other materials, though, didn't act the same way. The scientists chemically split things such as sugar, water, and salt into their smallest possible bits, and those bits did not act the same as miniature chunks of the larger pieces. Instead, the smallest bits of sugar, water, and salt acted like other elements.

Water

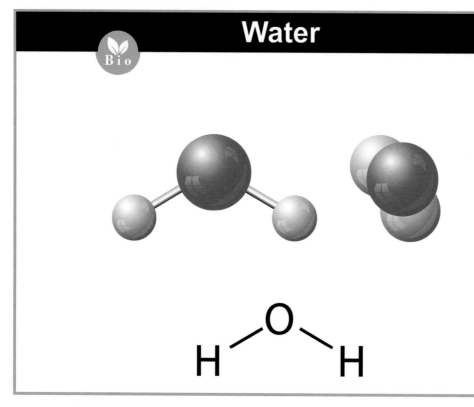

This image shows three different ways of representing a molecule of water. Water is composed of two atoms of hydrogen and one atom of oxygen. Scientists in the nineteenth century figured out that water and other molecules could be split into atoms, but they also thought those atoms could not be split into smaller pieces. Observations in the next decades would show that assumption was wrong.

Chemists realized that sugar, water, and salt are compounds composed of elements put together in very specific ratios. That is, table salt is made from equal numbers of atoms of sodium and chloride. Water has twice as many hydrogen atoms as it has atoms of oxygen. Table sugar is more complicated, with twice as much carbon as hydrogen and almost as much oxygen as carbon.

Chemists also figured out the weight of each of those atoms. Hydrogen atoms were lighter than carbon, which was lighter than oxygen, and so on. They could isolate the different elements— they could fill a jar with only oxygen or make a lump of only copper, for example—but they didn't know much else about atoms. To look at finer details, they needed to find a way to put more energy into these atoms.

In the middle of the 1800s, scientists already knew that electric charge was an important property of material, and they knew that positive and negative charges would attract each other, while two like charges repelled one another. They also knew that atoms were usually neutral—they showed no electric charge, but with some sort of special treatment, a neutral material could be made to show a charge. So maybe each atom was really two pieces put together, one with a positive charge and one with a negative charge. Because atoms were usually neutral, scientists knew the two pieces must find it very easy to come together, so if they were going to have any chance of seeing the pieces, they needed to put them in a vacuum, a volume almost empty of other particles.

ELECTRIC CHARGE

During the 1700s, scientists examined what happens when different materials, such as glass and silk, are rubbed together. It's the same effect that gives you a shock when you rub your feet against a

(continued on the next page)

(continued from previous page)

carpet and touch a piece of metal. The glass is left with something they called positive charge. They also discovered negative charge, and they learned that positive and negative charges attract one another.

With more investigation they determined that electric charge creates an electric field that sets up a voltage, or potential difference, that will make other charged particles move. That provided insight into the structure of matter, but it also helped scientists build new tools for further investigations.

So scientists built a device to split apart the two parts of an atom. It's called a Crookes' tube—a hollow glass tube with specially shaped pieces of metal inside.[1] Scientists pulled the air out of those tubes, making a vacuum. Hooked up to a voltage, those metal structures are called electrodes. Connected to a negative voltage, it's called a cathode, and connected to a positive voltage, it's called an anode. With a big negative voltage on the cathode and a big positive voltage on an anode, the atoms on the electrodes might be made to split into their two pieces.

And that's just what happened—kind of.

Something was split out from the cathode and would go through the vacuum in the tube and create a visible glow. J. J. Thomson (1856–1940), head of the Cavendish Laboratory at Cambridge University, did a set of experiments that showed the particles that split out were not "half atoms," but were much smaller. Those particles were electrons—tiny negatively charged particles.[2]

A Crookes' tube uses a very high voltage to pull apart the charged particles in atoms. Scientists had thought that atoms might be "half positive and half negative," but J J Thomson used a Crookes' tube to discover that the negative parts are far lighter and smaller than the complete atom.

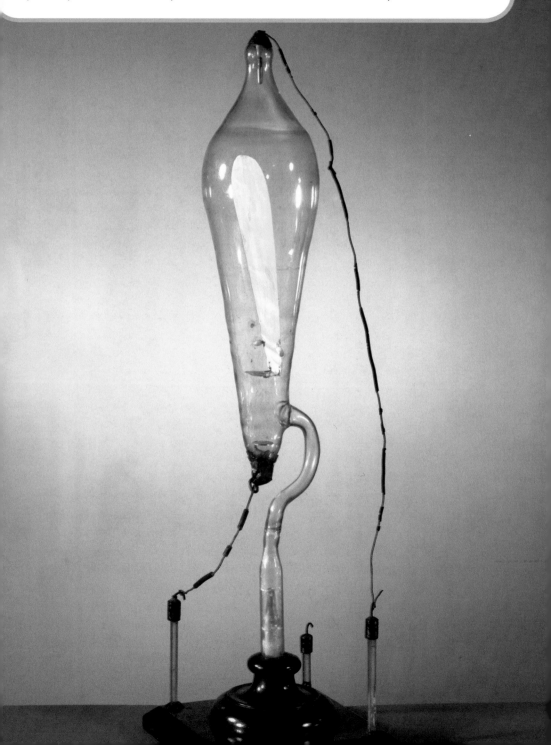

Finishing the Picture of the Atom

Scientists knew a few things about atoms: first, they were usually neutral. Second, they had some tiny negative particles in them. Third, the overall atoms were much heavier than the electrons that

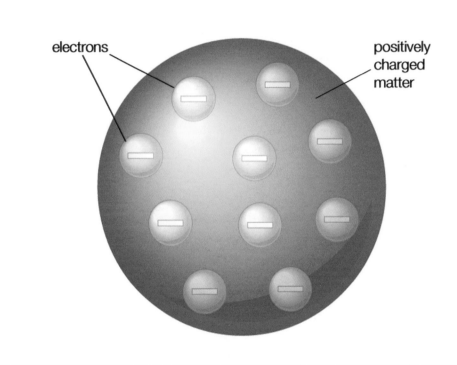

electrons

positively
charged
matter

Complete atoms usually don't react to an electric field (or voltage, which is just another way of thinking of an electric field). Because they don't react, they must not have a net charge. But when they're split apart, little negative bits fly out. 11 Thomson thought that must mean the negative bits were like raisins in a positive-dough raisin bread, or, in an image more familiar to the English of Thomson's time, like raisins in a plum pudding.

came out of them. Maybe atoms were like a "plum pudding"— a light, fluffy cake with raisins baked all throughout. The raisins were the negatively charged electrons and the fluffy cake was the positive part. In this picture, all matter would be built up from fluffy bricks stacked on top of one another, kind of like a building made of marshmallows packed together.

Imagine trying to find out what's inside a wall, but you have some constraints, some limitations. There are two open holes, one on either side of the wall, but you can't look inside or reach inside. You can, however, try to throw something through the hole in the wall. That's where scientists were in the early 1900s. They wanted to learn if their model of matter—that image of something like marshmallows stacked up—was the right one, but they couldn't look, they could only send something through it.

Ernest Rutherford (1871–1937), who eventually took over the Cavendish Laboratory after Thomson, had just the thing to throw through matter. His projectiles were called alpha particles, one of the particles that came out when atoms radioactively decayed. Alpha particles are thousands of times heavier than electrons, but they are still very small, meaning they are dense, positively charged objects.

Rutherford was expecting that his alpha particles would pretty much sail right through a thin sheet of gold foil, kind of like the way a rock from a slingshot would fly through that wall filled with marshmallows. And that's mostly what happened. But not completely. Every once in a while, one of the alpha particles would bounce right back. Rutherford said it was "as if you fired a 15-inch [38-centimeter] [artillery] shell at a piece of tissue paper and it came back and hit you."[3]

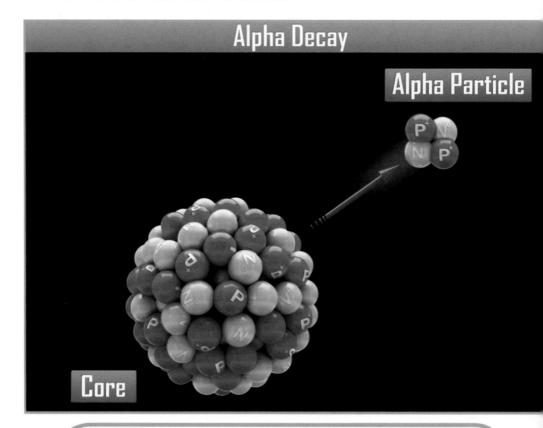

Alpha Decay

Alpha Particle

Core

Alpha particles are clumps of matter that burst away from certain atoms when they radioactively decay. They are positively charged and much heavier than atoms, so Rutherford expected alpha particles to fly right through other matter. When they didn't, he realized atoms must be different than what he expected.

This new information made scientists change their minds. Matter is not composed of a bunch of light, cakelike positive material sprinkled with negative raisinlike electrons. Instead, each atom has a tiny, dense, positive core, called the nucleus, surrounded by a bunch of even tinier electrons whirling around. Most of the space in an atom is empty, in the same way that the solar system has a big sun in the middle and small planets orbiting far away, separated by a lot of empty space.[4]

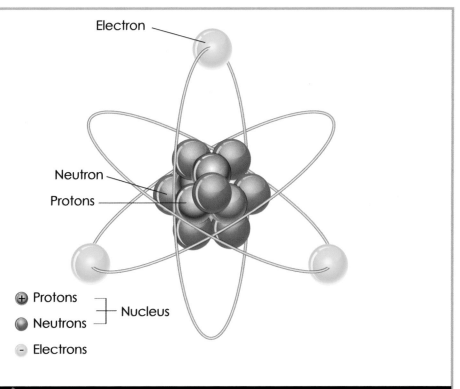

Electron

Neutron

Protons

⊕ Protons — Nucleus
🔴 Neutrons —
⊖ Electrons

 Biology

Atom Structure

This diagram represents an atom: a small, relatively heavy nucleus surrounded by light electrons whizzing around. But electrons are much farther from the nucleus than this drawing would make them seem.

Later experiments showed that the nucleus was itself composed of two different types of particles: protons and neutrons. Protons and neutrons are about two thousand times heavier than electrons. Protons have a positive charge that is equal and opposite to the charge of the electron, but neutrons have no net charge: they are neutral.

During all of this work, the experimental results were ahead of the understanding. In other words, experiment was ahead of theory. Each new experiment caused scientists to change their mental model of the atom.

It had to change because according to the theories of the time, electrons orbiting around a nucleus would lose energy pretty much every time the atom interacted with the outside world. Eventually all the electrons would collapse right down into the nucleus and there would be no atoms left. But atoms are there. The theory needed to change, and change in a big way.

The change that was coming was one of the largest in the history of science. It was the emergence of a new theory that predicted some strange, nearly unimaginable effects. It was a theory called quantum mechanics, and it would change the world.

A Strange New World

Rutherford's model of the atom—as a miniature solar system with the nucleus as the sun and electrons as the planets—presented a big problem. According to everything that scientists understood about how that system should work, it shouldn't! The theories said the orbiting electron should give up energy and spiral into the nucleus, never to be pried away. But that didn't happen. An atom could give away energy and take energy in, and it was still (usually) the same atom, with the same electron zipping around the same nucleus.

Other problems were coming up at the same time. There was a long list of measurements that didn't seem to make sense. Some of those measurements were of electrons as atoms absorbed light and escaped from a metal surface. Some were of the light that atoms emit as they get rid of extra energy. Even the red-hot and white-hot colors of a heated chunk of iron could not be explained with what scientists knew at the time.

Those observations had one thing in common: they all dealt with the way matter and energy act at the smallest levels. The

Energy Levels

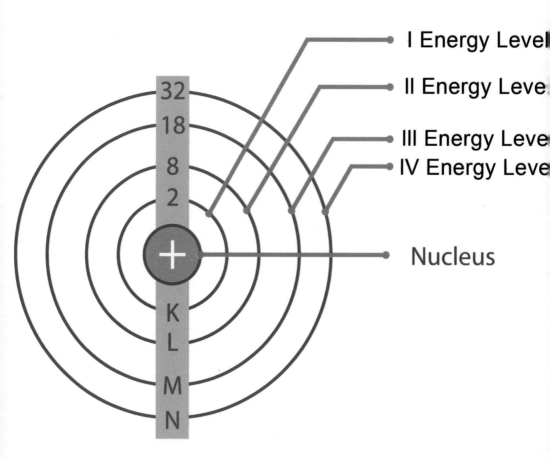

32
18
8
2

I Energy Level

II Energy Level

III Energy Level

IV Energy Level

Nucleus

K
L
M
N

A yo-yo can spin at any speed, and it can unroll all along a string. Extremely small objects, such as electrons in atoms, act differently. They can only spin at certain speeds and only whirl around in specific orbits. Electrons can only jump from one speed to the next and from one position to the next. This diagram illustrates the idea of electron energy levels in an atom.

old understanding, now called classical physics, is perfectly fine for understanding baseballs and planets, but it doesn't work for understanding atoms and molecules. This was really exciting because it meant the door was wide open for developing a new understanding.

This happens all the time in science. A theory explains a lot of observations that have already been made, so it seems to be pretty well supported. But then new observations come along, and they demand a new theory. The new theory has two jobs: first, to explain the new observations, and second, to give the same predictions as the previous theory for the old observations.[1] That's not an easy job, and it usually needs to be done in a few steps.

A new theory was needed to explain the behavior of atoms and molecules. That new theory came about, just as many new theories do, in small steps. The first step was to introduce the idea that, unlike a baseball, an electron could not have any amount of energy, but that tiny steps separate the energies it is allowed to have. That is, energy is "quantized."

A person can jog at a rate of 6 miles (9.65 kilometers) per hour, or 6.01 miles (9.67 km) per hour, or 6.2 miles (9.98 km) per hour, or any other speed they can reach. The idea of quantized energy is that an electron can't zip around at any speed, but it has to jump from one energy to another.

The difference between those energies is the quantum of energy for that system. Scientists recognized the importance of that idea, and they called their new theory quantum mechanics.[2]

The first steps toward quantum mechanics began to explain why atoms didn't all collapse into themselves. But those first steps would lead to some very strange predictions.

A Quantum Leap

Imagine a bowling ball rolling down the alley, headed for the pins. Just like the person jogging, that bowling ball can be tossed at any speed up to the limit of the bowler's strength. According to quantum mechanics, if that bowling ball were the size of an electron, that wouldn't be true. There could be, say, ten different allowed speeds.

The fastest speed would be perhaps something like 20 miles (32 km) per hour, the next highest possible speed would be something like 18 miles (29 km) per hour. That bowling ball would look pretty strange. It would start out at 20 miles per hour and keep going at that exact speed until it suddenly slowed down to 18 miles per hour, then 16 miles (26 km) per hour, and so on. Rather than smoothly getting slower, as normal bowling balls do, it would jerk as it rolled down the lane.

But that wouldn't be the strangest behavior of the electron-sized bowling ball.

The ball wouldn't be able to stay still. As strange as it seems, the slowest speed of the bowling ball would not be zero. The slowest it could go would still have it rolling down the alley, slowly.

Even that's not the strangest thing. The bowling ball can do one of two things: it can knock over some pins or it can miss all the pins and go in the gutter. There might be a 90 percent chance that some pins will go down and a 10 percent chance the ball ends up in the gutter. If the bowling ball were an electron it would do both—until the moment you look at it.

In the early 1900s, the Danish physicist Niels Bohr (1885–1962) pointed out that this was a big problem for quantum mechanics to deal with: the exact same experiment done one hundred times will not yield the same result.[3] It's not a problem with the experiment or the measurement; it's the microscopic particles themselves.

If you roll the bowling ball and then turn around to eat some nachos, your electron-sized bowling ball has done both things: 90 percent of it has knocked down some pins, and 10 percent of it has ended up in the gutter. As soon as you look at it, only one of those options will be true. On average, nine times out of ten you can turn around and see the ball has knocked down some pins, and one time out of ten you will see it hasn't hit any pins.

It's as if the bowling ball were spread out into all the possible places it could be—until the moment you look at it, when it can only be in one place.

Those are all very strange ways for a bowling ball to act, but they aren't strange ways for an electron to act. That's one reason quantum mechanics is so difficult to understand: objects that are extremely small act differently from any object we directly encounter. When scientists say something like, "Imagine an electron is like a tiny bead circling around an orange," it might help to create an image of an atom, but it's not really what's going on.

The electron isn't a bead (no matter how small a bead you imagine). The electron is something fuzzy, something that moves on many different paths all at once, until it interacts with something else when it may become localized. If, for example, the bowling ball had knocked down the number 3, 6, and 10 pins, then the interaction with those pins would have localized the ball to the right side of the bowling lane. But before it's localized, that electron-sized bowling ball would have been spread out all over the lane.

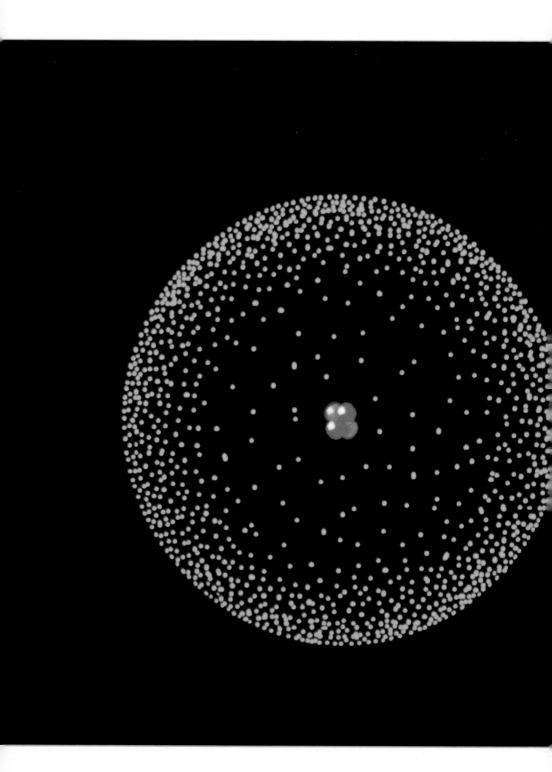

This illustration shows the idea that electrons act differently from familiar objects. Although helium atoms, like this one, only have two electrons, each of those electrons acts as if it is in many places at once—until it interacts with something else. Then the electrons have to more or less "pick a spot."

When scientists come up with a theory that is so different from anything else, they are very reluctant to accept it. So why do scientists believe in quantum mechanics? Because it has successfully explained starlight and artificial light, particle motion in a magnetic field, current in tiny integrated circuits, and many other otherwise unexplainable behaviors.

Scientists didn't make up the rules of quantum mechanics to make the world more complicated; they came up with quantum mechanics to explain observations in the simplest possible way. In a 1990 paper, "The Stability of Matter," Elliot Lieb (1932–), an American mathematical physicist, wrote, "As far as we know today [quantum mechanics] is capable of explaining everything about ordinary matter . . . with stunning numerical accuracy."[4]

SPECIAL RELATIVITY

About the same time as unexpected observations were driving the new theory of quantum mechanics, other observations were driving a new theory called special relativity. Measurements in the late 1800s, primarily on traveling light waves, had shown that another theory of physics, the electromagnetic theory, also wasn't quite right. Albert Einstein (1879–1955) took a look at the problems and realized they could be solved if we assume that everyone would always measure the same speed of light, no matter how fast they were moving.[5]

That's the foundation for a theory called special relativity. Special relativity leads to Einstein's famous $E=mc^2$ equation. To get to the equation that predicted the existence of antimatter, English theoretical physicist Paul Dirac (1902–1984) combined results from special relativity with quantum mechanics.

This drawing shows one of Einstein's famous thought experiments. In the top part of the image, the arrow shot from the train would arrive at the target first because the train's speed and the arrow's speed add together. The two beams of light, however, would arrive at the target at the same time. That's Einstein's "special relativity" theory, and, although it's strange, it turns out to be right.

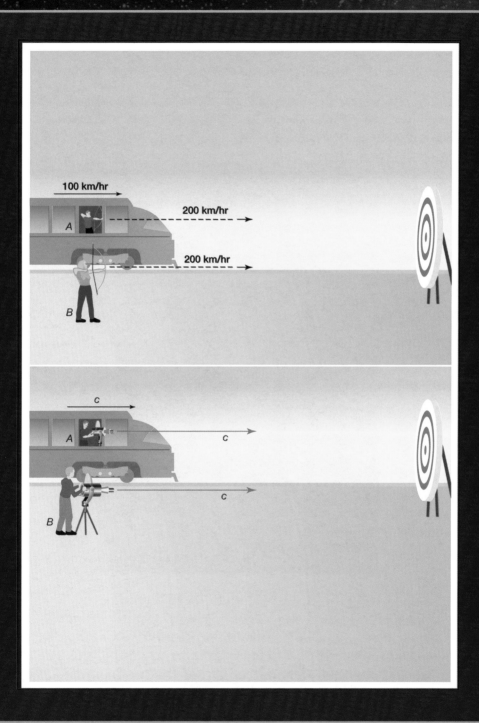

An Even Stranger Prediction

From the late 1800s through the early 1900s, scientists had been presented with a whole slew of strange observations. The theory of quantum mechanics described them all. So although quantum mechanics painted a pretty strange picture, it did such a good

In the early twentieth century, Paul Dirac combined ideas from two different (and oddly peculiar) theories: quantum mechanics and special relativity. He showed that the two theories together predicted there should be an "antielectron," a particle equal and opposite to the electron. Most scientists thought there must be some mistake, but just a few years later, the antielectron was discovered.

job of explaining the world of small particles that scientists were willing to take the strange with the good. But now they were going to be asked to accept even stranger things.

A scientific theory doesn't just explain observations; it presents a model of how the world works. Theories in physics are usually mathematical models of the world, so scientists can look at equations and get an idea of how the world works. When—as in the case of quantum mechanics—the equations describe a lot of behavior that has been seen, scientists are very confident the theory is fairly accurate. But when a theory predicts things that have never been seen, it can be pretty tough to stay confident in it.

In 1928, Paul Dirac worked through some equations of quantum mechanics and made a startling prediction. He found that the exact same equations that described the electron and its properties also described a matched opposite: a particle that was almost a twin of the electron, but with a positive charge instead of a negative charge.

Scientists had just gotten used to the idea of electrons and protons, and those particles had been seen. In the hundreds of experiments that had been done by 1928, scientists had seen uncountable billions of electrons. No one had ever seen this "antielectron." Many scientists thought Dirac had gone too far— that he was exaggerating the importance of the equations and using them in places where they didn't really apply.

Those doubters were about to be proven wrong in a spectacular way.

Something from Nothing

The years around the turn of the twentieth century, from the late 1890s to the early 1900s, were a time of rapid discovery. In addition to Thomson's and Rutherford's discoveries about electrons and atoms, Henri Becquerel (1852–1908) and Marie Curie (1867–1934) had discovered and explored a new phenomenon: radioactivity.

Around that same time, other important work was being done. Albert Einstein was looking at new observations and tying them in to a new physical theory. One result of his new theory was his most famous equation, $E=mc^2$. The next steps in the understanding of antimatter relied on both that famous equation and the discovery of radioactivity.

When radioactivity was discovered, only one thing was known for sure: that certain atoms give off some form of high energy. Becquerel discovered radioactivity when he had left some photographic plates next to some chemical salts in a dark drawer. When Becquerel developed the photographs, it appeared as if light had hit the film. It wasn't light, but other energy from atoms in the salts. Later on it would be discovered that the radioactive energy mostly came in three different forms: alpha, beta, and gamma rays. Those are just different particles of energy that leave certain atoms from time to time, changing the atom they leave behind.

The important thing for antimatter is that the interest in radioactivity got people interested in new methods of detection. One of those methods was the electroscope, in which two pieces of thin metal foil would start out separated from one another, but collapse against each other when exposed to radioactive energy. Another instrument was the cloud chamber. Cloud chambers are filled with vapor (usually water vapor) that is just on the edge of condensing, like rain. Radioactivity going through a cloud chamber triggers condensation just along the trail of the radioactive particle. A picture of the condensation trails is a picture of the path of the radioactive particles.[1]

Those were important tools in the search for knowledge of antimatter, but there was also an important theoretical understanding that needed to come into play.

Sooner or later everyone sees Einstein's famous equation, $E=mc^2$. This is what it means: E represents energy and c represents the speed of light (a very large number). When c is squared, the very large number becomes a huge number. The m represents mass, which is more or less how much something weighs. Put together, Einstein's equation says something like, "The energy of a particle is equal to its mass multiplied by a really big number." So Einstein's equation says a tiny bit of mass contains a lot of energy.

But Einstein's equation says more than that. It says that energy and mass are equal, that is, they are the same thing. So,

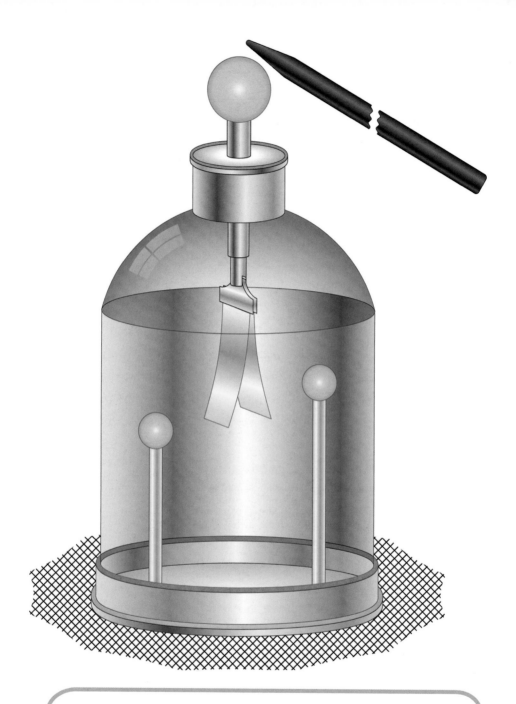

An electroscope is prepared by putting some electric charges on two thin gold leaves. The leaves will stay separated for a long time, unless other charges come along. Radioactive decay releases electric charges, so the electroscope can be used as a radioactivity detector.

as far as the universe is concerned, a certain amount of mass can be replaced by the corresponding larger amount of energy and nothing in the universe will be messed up. There are a few more pieces to that story, but the important part is that matter and energy are just different ways of looking at the same thing.

That theory, along with the electroscope and cloud chamber, prepared the way for scientists to discover antimatter.

Invisible Rays from the Sky

Soon after the discovery of radiation and the development of new detection tools, scientists noticed that there was background radiation everywhere. This made some sense because they knew radiation came from different soils and rocks, so it seemed logical that radiation from the soil and rock might come up from the earth and into the laboratory.

Put that way, it makes sense that the radiation would be strongest close to Earth and then weaken with distance away from the surface. And that's almost what happens.

In 1911, physicist Victor Hess (1883–1964) started a series of balloon flights to investigate how the strength of background radiation changed with altitude. He found that the radiation decreased as his balloon initially left the surface of Earth, but then it increased as the balloon continued to rise. All the way up to a height above more than three miles (higher than five kilometers) the radiation increased. This was puzzling because there were no soil or rocks high in the atmosphere; the higher a balloon went, the farther it was away from the known sources of radiation.

There was one other known energy source that floods Earth with energy all day, every day: the sun. Perhaps that high altitude

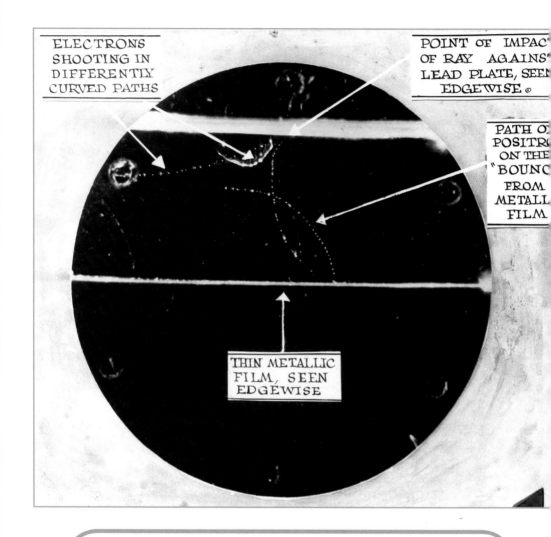

ELECTRONS
SHOOTING IN
DIFFERENTLY
CURVED PATHS

POINT OF IMPACT
OF RAY AGAINST
LEAD PLATE, SEEN
EDGEWISE

PATH OF
POSITRO
ON THE
"BOUNC
FROM
METALL
FILM

THIN METALLIC
FILM, SEEN
EDGEWISE

This photograph was taken at the California Institute of Technology in 1933. These little traces of condensed water show where energetic particles traveled through a chamber full of mist. The direction of the curve shows whether the particle is negative or positive. Some of these traces curve in opposite directions, showing that electrons are present, and also showing the presence of an antielectron, a positron.

radiation was coming from the sun. But then Hess took a balloon flight on the day of April 17, 1912—the day of a solar eclipse. The high-altitude radiation was just as strong during an eclipse. All of Hess's evidence combined to indicate that the radiation came from far distances in the universe. The particles of radiation were cosmic rays.[2]

That's important because the next step in the surprising history of antimatter came during the search to understand cosmic rays.

In 1932, California Institute of Technology researcher Carl Anderson (1905–1991) was using a cloud chamber to investigate cosmic rays. His cloud chamber was placed in a magnetic field because charged particles will take a winding, curling path in a magnetic field. The direction of the curl indicates the sign of the charge—negative or positive, or, if the particle is neutral, no bending at all. The length of the path is related to the energy and size of the particle.

During the summer, Anderson looked at thirteen hundred photographs of energetic particles. Fifteen of those showed something that had never been seen before: a particle the size of an electron, but with a *positive* charge. The only known single particle with a positive charge was the proton, but the proton was nearly two thousand times as heavy as the electron. Anderson's particle was exactly like an electron, except that it had the opposite charge.

Anderson had discovered an *anti*electron, a particle he called the "positron." Quite logically, Anderson suggested that the electron should be renamed the "negatron," but that suggestion was not adopted. But Anderson's main conclusion could not be ignored. He had discovered antimatter.[3]

ANTIMATTER INSIDE US

Positrons, or antielectrons, are not just produced by cosmic rays; they also appear as the product of some radioactive decay. Specially prepared oxygen atoms, for example, can change into atoms of nitrogen. As they transform they release a positron. If those positrons are around other atoms they will almost immediately bump into electrons. When they do, each positron and electron will annihilate, releasing a wave of energy.

To stay in balance, the wave must have two parts heading off in opposite directions, and the energy of each part must equal the mass of the electron times the speed of light squared, as in Einstein's equation. Positron emission tomography (PET) is a medical imaging technique that puts something like those special oxygen atoms at a problem spot in the body. Then PET detects those two waves of energy that come from the annihilating electron and positron.[4]

Positrons might seem like things that have no connection to ordinary life, but every day positrons are used in hospitals around the world. In positron emission tomography, a patient gets an injection of material that will release positrons. The positrons quickly crash into electrons and release a very specific amount of energy in the form of a gamma ray. The gamma ray detector creates an image of where the positrons came from.

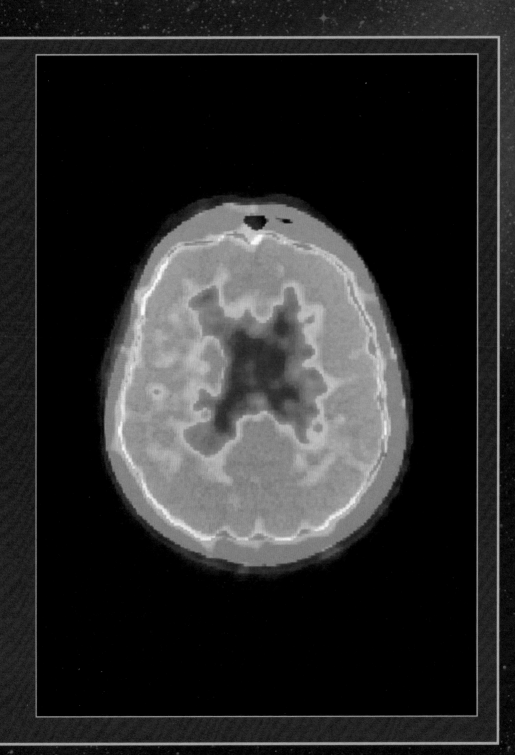

The Theoretical Side

Dirac's interpretation of his equation that predicted the existence of the antielectron was not immediately accepted. Some scientists thought there was a mistake, and some thought it a sign the mathematics of quantum mechanics was not completely accurate. The biggest reason for that skepticism was that no one had then seen an antielectron.

But now Anderson had seen one. The main objection to Dirac's prediction was now gone. Other scientists began to investigate the equation and its implications. There are many complicated levels to the equation, but they can be broadly understood by

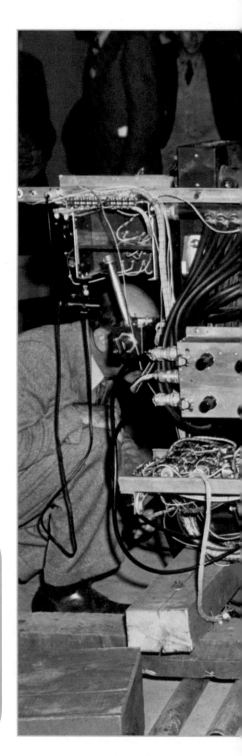

Carl Anderson explains his cloud chamber to journalists in 1946. Anderson's discovery of the antielectron while using a cloud chamber to do cosmic ray research confirmed Dirac's prediction that the negatively charged electron had a positively charged counterpart.

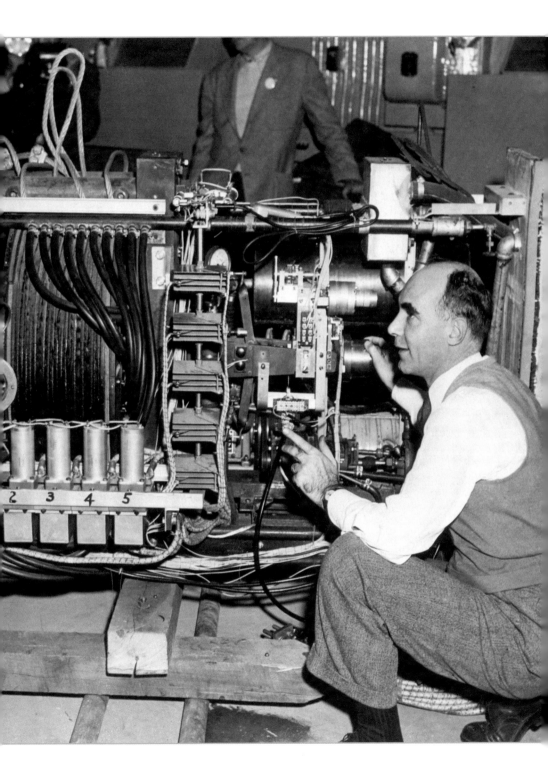

going back to Einstein's famous equation: $E=mc^2$. That equation says that energy and mass are just different ways of looking at the same thing.

That means a particle with a certain energy could evaporate into a burst of X-rays, for example, with the same total energy. That is, the change from matter to energy wouldn't break any of the rules for how particles act. But there's a little more to the story.

Consider, for example, an electron at rest, that is, not moving. That electron could disappear, leaving a burst of gamma ray energy with a little more than five hundred thousand electron volts. Einstein's equation would perfectly balance out. The problem, though, is that the electron has charge, and there's a separate rule in the universe that charge can neither be created nor destroyed. Put another way, the total charge of a system cannot change. The electron has a negative charge. It can't transform into a burst of gamma ray energy because gamma rays don't have any charge. The charge at the end would be different than it was at the beginning, and the net charge can't change, so that electron all by itself can't transform into a burst of gamma ray energy.

But if that electron has an antielectron, a positron, nearby, then the two can crash together. The electron has a negative charge and the positron has a positive charge, so the total charge at the beginning is zero. When a positron and electron come together, they will destroy themselves, leaving behind that burst of energy, and still no net charge. There are a few other quantities that must be the same before and after an interaction—that is, there are certain things that are in balance before an interaction and must still be in balance after the interaction.

The point is that an electron and a positron are the opposite of one another. That is, they are perfectly balanced. When they destroy each other, as long as the total energy afterward matches Einstein's equation, everything that needs to stay in balance will automatically still be in balance.

There is another strange prediction of quantum mechanics: in the same way that two particles can crash together, leaving behind a burst of energy, a burst of energy can create two particles—as long as everything is in balance between those two particles. An electron and a positron are kind of opposite twins, so they automatically balance each other out. That means electrons and positrons can just appear out of empty space, as long as there is enough energy.

An electron and a positron—a particle and its matched antiparticle—can pop up out of almost nothing. And a particle and antiparticle can destroy one another completely, leaving no trace other than the wave of energy that zips away from the point of destruction.

Are there other antiparticle pairs out there, popping in and out of existence?

Chapter Five

Building Antimatter

Imagine you set up a soccer game at the park with some friends. But no one has remembered to bring a ball. There's nothing to do except send someone home to grab one. If the rules of physics for soccer balls were something like the rules for electrons, then there would be another option. The group could get together and yell, and as long as they put enough energy into the yelling, some of that energy could go into creating a "soccer ball" and an "anti-soccer ball."

To keep things balanced, the two balls would have to appear moving exactly away from each other at the exact same speed. Since there was no charge to start with, the two soccer balls would either have to have equal and opposite charges or be uncharged (that is, neutral). Of course, the total energy of the yelling would have to be equal to the speed of light squared multiplied by twice the mass of a soccer ball (that's from Einstein's equation describing how matter and energy are equivalent). And you'd have to be really careful to keep the soccer ball and the anti-soccer ball away from one another, because if they came too close they would destroy themselves in a burst of energy as loud as what the group did to make them appear.

Now imagine that the energy to make two soccer balls appear is much larger than you can produce by all yelling together. How would you investigate everything about soccer balls and anti-soccer balls? You'd do something like wait for a thunderstorm, when the energy released by the clap of thunder would perhaps be enough to create soccer balls for a whole tournament.

That would be a little inconvenient.

That's similar to the situation in the early 1900s. Scientists had learned that a wave of energy could create electrons and positrons, but to see that creation they needed to wait for the right circumstances to come around. Even then they needed a little luck to be able to catch the measurement they were looking for. Those difficulties meant that it was hard to get new experimental results. But that didn't mean they stopped working on the problem.

Crushing Matter

Scientists were getting a lot of information from particles emerging from radioactively decaying atoms. That's how Rutherford and his colleagues discovered the nucleus, by using alpha particles from natural radioactive decay. Rutherford's alpha particles, though, bounced right back when they hit the nucleus of an atom. The next step was to crash into the target nuclei so strongly that the nuclei would break apart. Natural radioactivity wasn't strong enough, and waiting around for cosmic rays wasn't reliable enough. Scientists needed new tools. Those new tools came in the form of particle accelerators.

Particle accelerators are machines that use electric fields to push charged particles along a designated path. They also use magnetic fields to keep those particles on the path. The first particle accelerators could fit on a tabletop, but the largest one now is a ring more than 16 miles (27 km) around.[1,2] These machines have one job: to speed up particles so fast that they can rip apart target particles. That's kind of like making a basketball go fast enough to shatter a wall into bricks flying in different directions.

The experiments done with these particle accelerators, along with lots of work on mathematical theories, have revealed that positrons, antielectrons, are not the only antiparticles. In fact, every particle has an antiparticle. So how many different types of particles and antiparticles are in the universe?

THE ANTIPROTON DECELERATOR

The largest particle accelerator in the world is at CERN, the European Laboratory for Nuclear Physics in Geneva, Switzerland. CERN hosts the largest machine ever built, the Large Hadron Collider (LHC). The LHC and other accelerators at CERN work by making particles move very fast—almost as fast as light itself. When that fast beam crashes into a target, it releases so much energy that all sorts of particles and antiparticles are created. But to keep everything in balance, those end particles have to be moving fast, too.

To make antiprotons stick around a while longer, researchers at CERN had to build a decelerator—a machine to slow particles down. The Antiproton Decelerator slows protons down so they can be trapped and examined in more detail.[3]

The Large Hadron Collider at CERN is the biggest machine ever built. It accelerates particles to extremely high speeds and crashes them into other particles. The resulting energy burst creates pairs of particles and antiparticles. Today scientists at CERN are studying those antiparticles in more detail.

The electron was the first discovered, but protons were not far behind. Electrons have a negative charge and protons have an equal and opposite positive charge. Protons, though, are about two thousand times heavier than electrons. The simplest atom, hydrogen, just has one electron zipping around one proton. All other atoms have another particle in the nucleus: the neutron. The neutron and proton weigh almost exactly the same, but the neutron has no charge. So at first there were just electrons, protons, and neutrons, and antiparticles for each of them.

Scientists working at accelerators (and using cosmic rays) revealed a picture of a whole set of other particles.

Electrons, as far as we can tell, cannot be broken apart. They are a type of particle called a lepton. Other leptons are the muon and the tau particle, along with three types of a different particle called a neutrino.

Protons and neutrons are a different type of particle called hadrons, and hadrons can be broken apart. They can be broken into particles called quarks. If we call the electron charge -1, then the proton charge is +1. But it turns out that the proton is made of three quarks tightly connected to each other. A quark called an up, with a charge of +2/3, and a quark called a down, with a charge of -1/3, and one more up quark finish off the set. The charges add up, $+2/3 + +2/3 + -1/3 = +1$, just as observed. The neutron is also comprised of three quarks, two downs and one up. Together their charges are $-1/3 + -1/3 + +2/3 = 0$, which is what it is observed to be.

Experiments at higher energies have revealed many other particles, each of them made of other combinations of quarks. Scientists put all those observations together and realized there are four other quarks, called strange, charm, top, and bottom. When that whole picture is put together all those particles fit into

MATTER
from molecule to quark

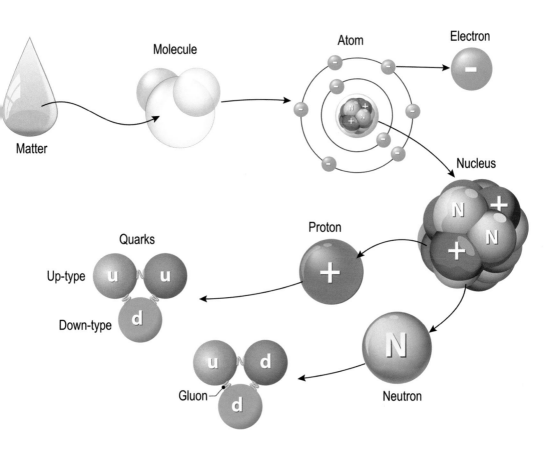

This picture shows how mental models of the universe have developed through the ages. First, some philosophers thought all matter was composed of water, but then observations revealed water itself is composed of molecules, each molecule consisting of two atoms of hydrogen and one of oxygen. Then atoms themselves were shown to consist of electrons, neutrons, and protons. Now we know neutrons and protons are composed of even smaller particles called quarks.

what's called the standard model of particle physics.[4] There are twelve elementary particles in the standard model, and every one of them has an antiparticle.

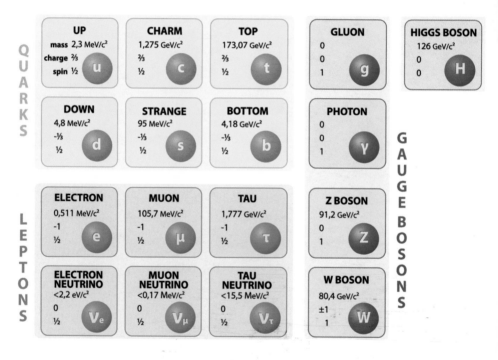

STANDARD MODEL OF ELEMENTARY PARTICLES

QUARKS

UP
mass 2,3 MeV/c²
charge ⅔
spin ½
u

CHARM
1,275 GeV/c²
⅔
½
c

TOP
173,07 GeV/c²
⅔
½
t

DOWN
4,8 MeV/c²
-⅓
½
d

STRANGE
95 MeV/c²
-⅓
½
s

BOTTOM
4,18 GeV/c²
-⅓
½
b

LEPTONS

ELECTRON
0,511 MeV/c²
-1
½
e

MUON
105,7 MeV/c²
-1
½
μ

TAU
1,777 GeV/c²
-1
½
τ

ELECTRON NEUTRINO
<2,2 eV/c²
0
½
Vₑ

MUON NEUTRINO
<0,17 MeV/c²
0
½
Vμ

TAU NEUTRINO
<15,5 MeV/c²
0
½
Vτ

GLUON
0
0
1
g

PHOTON
0
0
1
γ

Z BOSON
91,2 GeV/c²
0
1
Z

W BOSON
80,4 GeV/c²
±1
1
W

HIGGS BOSON
126 GeV/c²
0
0
H

GAUGE BOSONS

The current understanding of matter reveals that everything is made of twelve fundamental matter particles (six types of quarks and six types of leptons). Each of those twelve has an antiparticle. The gauge bosons and Higgs boson are kind of like the energy that glues the matter particles together. These gluelike particles don't have antiparticles.

Creating Antimatter

All the elementary particles in the standard model are very small, which means they follow the rules for small particles. That is, they follow the rules of quantum mechanics. There are some other complicated rules, too, but the important point is that as long as other things are in balance, energy can change into particles and particles can change into energy.

Matter and Antimatter Atoms

+ ● Proton
○ ● Neutron
− ● Electron

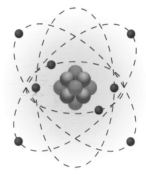

− ● Antiproton
○ ● Antineutron
+ ● Positron

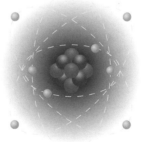

Matter and antimatter are almost exactly alike. From a distance, they're almost impossible to tell apart because every particle is replaced by its twin antiparticle. If matter and antimatter atoms are brought together, though, they will destroy each other in a burst of energy!

Empty space has no charge. So any particles that are created must also have no total charge. For example, if there is a particle with a +1 charge created, then there must be a particle with -1 charge. There are some other quantities that must be in balance too, but it's the same principle.

But what is an antiparticle? It's a perfect equal and opposite twin of the normal particle. That means it weighs exactly the same amount but everything else is opposite. Think about, then, what happens when there's enough energy around to create two antiparticles. That is, in terms of Einstein's famous equation, $E = mc^2 + mc^2 = 2mc^2$. Because the energy is enough for that equation to be true, there is just as much energy before the particles are created as there is after.

What about all the other things that must be balanced, the charge and some other quantities? Well, a particle and an antiparticle are exact opposites, so if they are created together, all of those things that must be in balance are automatically in balance. So creating matter should be as straightforward as building up energy and watching the pairs of particles and antiparticles appear.

And that's just about what happens. But then what follows?

Chapter
Six

Antimatter and the Big Bang

The accepted theories of physics say that matter and antimatter particles are perfect opposites. That is, they have the same mass, but they are exactly opposite in every other way. But scientists already know that the accepted theories will have to be modified a little bit. That's because they explain a lot of the observations, but not quite everything. To figure out how the existing theories should be modified, scientists need to look at more antimatter.

There's a problem, though. Antimatter particles don't stick around. They quickly find an opposite and annihilate. To measure the properties of antiparticles, scientists have to keep those antiparticles around for a while.

Holding On

Around the beginning of the twenty-first century, scientists working at CERN were making antiprotons by putting a lot of energy into a collision. They found one way to hold on to them, using ready-made holders: atoms.

Helium atoms have a nucleus of two positively charged protons and two neutral neutrons surrounded by two negatively charged electrons. Those electrons are held in place because the positive charge of the nucleus attracts the negative charge of the electrons. In the early 2000s, an experiment at CERN sent negatively charged antiprotons into a bunch of helium molecules, where an antiproton could knock out one of the electrons in the helium molecule and take its place. That made antiprotons hang around about a thousand times longer, but still only for a few millionths of a second.[1]

About ten years later, a different experiment at CERN created antihydrogen atoms. Where a hydrogen atom has a positive proton surrounded by a negative electron, antihydrogen has a negative antiproton surrounded by a positive positron. Scientists started by holding on to those antihydrogen atoms for a few thousandths of a second, but they quickly improved their method to be able to hold on to these antiatoms for more than fifteen minutes.[2]

So far, none of these researchers have reported any difference between particles and their opposite twin antiparticles. Why is that important? Three reasons: first, because any difference would provide information to modify the current theories about particles and energy; second, because our universe appears to be made of matter with a very small amount of antimatter; and third, because we have to understand antimatter if we ever want to use it as a fuel.

What Antimatter Tells Us

Current physics theories say that particles can materialize and disappear as long as the amount of energy stays the same before and after the change, and as long as certain other quantities also stay the same. Although we have not discussed the whole list of quantities, the idea is the same as with charge. There can't be any change in the amount of net charge after transforming from energy to particle or particle to energy.

The other quantities that need to be balanced are things such as magnetic moment, momentum, lepton number, and quark number. The details are not important to a basic understanding; what is important is that all of those quantities are automatically evened out when a particle and its companion antiparticle are involved.

There are two ways that could be wrong. First, maybe antiparticles aren't completely perfect opposites of each other. Second, maybe it turns out that not every one of those quantities always need to be in balance. Either way it would mean that something in the current understanding is wrong. So far, no observations have shown either one of those two things are wrong.

But scientists know there's something they don't quite understand.

To understand the problem, think about the beginning of the universe. The universe started with the big bang—something like a giant explosion of energy. With all that energy around, all sorts of particle/antiparticle pairs would have been created. At first, all the particles would be crammed so tightly together that

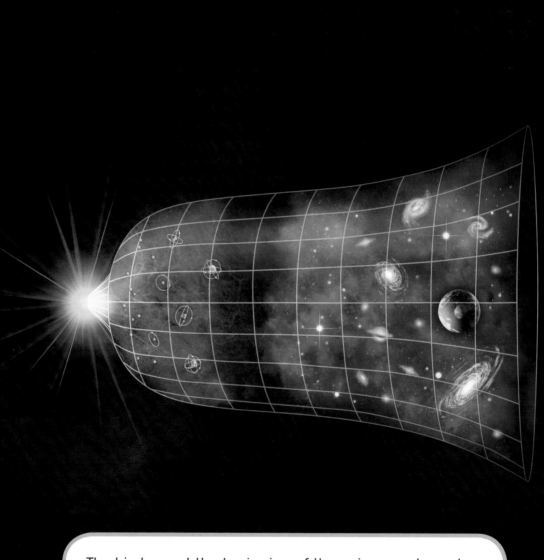

The big bang at the beginning of the universe released an incredible amount of energy. That surge of energy should have created just as many antiparticles as particles. But today's universe seems to be made of far more matter than antimatter. As of right now, no one knows why.

they would destroy one another and turn right back into energy. Eventually, the universe would spread out and cool down enough that the particles would stick around. But there should be just as many antiparticles as particles. So why does our universe have lots of matter and hardly any antimatter?

So far no one knows.

That's one reason why scientists are so interested in creating, storing, and studying antimatter. Another reason is more practical, at least in a small way.

POWERING THE PLANETS

We are a long way from being able to harness antimatter, but the idea of using antimatter for energy came soon after antimatter was discovered. One early example was a set of stories written by science fiction author Jack Williamson (1908–2006). He wrote the stories in the 1930s and 1940s and later reworked them into a couple of novels. Williamson's books are built around the idea of using "contraterrene" asteroids as fuel for nearly unlimited power.

Williamson's books are fiction, but they identified two key concepts. First, antimatter and matter in contact will destroy one another and release energy. Second, there is no known reason for

(continued on the next page)

ASTOUNDING

SCIENCE-FICTION

A STREET & SMITH PUBLICATION

FEB. 1939

20¢

CRUCIBLE OF POWER   By Jack Williamson

(continued from page 67)

the universe to not have a lot of antimatter. So far, though, we haven't found any antimatter asteroids, and without a source of cheap, plentiful antimatter, Williamson's particular future will have to wait.

This February 1939 issue of *Astounding Science-Fiction* shows an illustration for Jack Williamson's story "The Crucible of Power." Williamson wrote about antimatter atoms—something he called by the made up word *contraterrene*—soon after antimatter was discovered. Williamson realized that the explosion created when matter and antimatter came together could be dangerous, but also that it could be harnessed to provide nearly unlimited energy if there were lots of antimatter around.

In general, fuels such as gasoline provide energy from chemical reactions. The amount of energy from a chemical reaction is much smaller than what can be released from the complete annihilation of a particle/antiparticle pair. Right now, that's not a practical idea because it's difficult and expensive to make antimatter and even harder and more costly to store it.

Antimatter fuels are far in the future, but even if it never happens, the study of antimatter can reveal fascinating hidden secrets of our universe.

CHAPTER NOTES

Chapter 1.
Asking the Right Questions

1. David C. Lindberg, *The Beginnings of Western Science* (Chicago, IL: The University of Chicago Press, 2007), p. 82.
2. *Internet Encyclopedia of Philosophy*, s.v. "Empedocles," accessed March 3, 2018, http://www.iep.utm.edu/empedocl/#SH4b.
3. Lindberg, pp. 80–90.
4. Richard Gaughan, *Accidental Genius: The World's Greatest By-Chance Discoveries* (New York, NY: Metro Books, 2010), pp. 26–29.
5. Elizabeth H. Oakes, *The Encyclopedia of World Scientists* (New York, NY: Infobase Publishing, 2007) pp. 86, 262–263.
6. Gregory J. Feist, *The Psychology of Science and the Origins of the Scientific Mind* (New Haven, CT: Yale University Press, 2006), pp. 9–12.

Chapter 2.
Finding the Atom

1. "Crookes' Tubes," Cathode Ray Tube Site, accessed March 3, 2018, https://www.crtsite.com/page7-4.html.
2. Isobel Falconer, "J. J. Thomson and the Discovery of the Electron," *Physics Education* 32 no. 4 (1997), p. 226.
3. American Physical Society, "May, 1911: Rutherford and the Discovery of the Atomic Nucleus," APS News, May 2006, https://www.aps.org/publications/apsnews/200605/history.cfm.

4. American Institute of Physics, "Alpha Particles and the Atom," Rutherford's Nuclear World, accessed March 3, 2018, https://history.aip.org/exhibits/rutherford/sections/alpha-particles-atom.html.

Chapter 3.
A Strange New World

1. "Even Theories Change," Understanding Science, accessed March 3, 2018, https://undsci.berkeley.edu/article/_0_0/howscienceworks_20.
2. Max Jammer, *The Conceptual Development of Quantum Mechanics* (New York, NY: American Institute of Physics, 1989), pp. 73–86.
3. Dipankar Home, *Conceptual Foundations of Quantum Physics* (New York, NY: Plenum Press, 1997), pp. 16–17.
4. Elliott H. Lieb, "The Stability of Matter: From Atoms to Stars," *Bulletin of the American Mathematical Society* 22 no.1 (1990), p. 1.
5. Domenico Giulini, *Special Relativity: A First Encounter* (Oxford, UK: Oxford University Press, 2005), pp. 28–41.

Chapter 4.
Something from Nothing

1. F. N. Flakus, "Detecting and Measuring Ionizing Radiation—A Short History," *IAEA Bulletin* 23 no. 4, International Atomic Energy Agency, accessed April 6, 2018, https://www.iaea.org/sites/default/files/publications/magazines/bulletin/bull23-4/23405043136.pdf.
2. Michael Friedlander, "A Century of Cosmic Rays," *Nature* 483 (March 22, 2012), pp. 400-401.

3. Eugene Cowan, "The Picture That Was Not Reversed," *Engineering and Science* 46 no. 2 (November 1982), pp. 6–10, 28.
4. Rachel A. Powsner, Matthew R. Palmer, and Edward R. Powsner, *Essentials of Nuclear Medicine Physics and Instrumentation* (Oxford, UK: Wiley-Blackwell, 2013), pp. 103–116.

Chapter 5.
Building Antimatter

1. Andrew Robert Steere, "A Timeline of Major Particle Accelerators" (thesis, Michigan State University, 2005), pp. 2–15.
2. "The Large Hadron Collider," CERN, accessed March 10, 2018, https://home.cern/topics/large-hadron-collider.
3. "The Antiproton Decelerator," CERN, accessed March 11, 2018, https://home.cern/about/accelerators/antiproton -decelerator.
4. Gregory Choppin et al., *Radiochemistry and Nuclear Chemistry* (Oxford, UK: Academic Press, 2013), pp. 15–29.

Chapter 6.
Antimatter and the Big Bang

1. Richard Gaughan, "Unique Atomic Spectroscopy Aims at Answering a Universal Question," *Spectroscopy* 18 no. 1 (January 2003), pp. 32–36.
2. John Matson, "Stick Up: Antimatter Atoms Trapped for More Than 15 Minutes," *Scientific American*, June 5, 2011, https://www.scientificamerican.com/article/antiatoms- alpha-1000-seconds/.

GLOSSARY

accelerator A machine with electric and magnetic fields designed to push tiny particles to very high speeds.

alpha particle/alpha ray One of the particles that can result from the radioactive decay of an atom. It consists of two protons and two neutrons.

annihilation The complete transformation of mass to energy, occurring when a particle and its antiparticle meet. The particles disappear and are replaced by an energy burst.

antiparticle The opposite to a primary particle.

beta particle/beta ray One of the particles that can result from the radioactive decay of an atom. It is the same thing as an electron.

big bang An unimaginably large burst of energy in which the entire universe was created.

cloud chamber A detection instrument that creates visible tracks when energetic charged particles travel through the chamber.

contraterrene An invented word in a fictional story meaning antimatter, or related to antimatter.

cosmic ray High energy particles from distant places in the universe, which enter Earth's atmosphere.

Crookes' tube A small glass tube with metal electrodes from which most of the air has been removed. It is a source of electrons.

electron A light, negatively charged particle that cannot be divided. It is a lepton.

electroscope A detection device that consists of two charged thin metal plates. The plates repel one another, but in the presence of radiation, they will quickly approach one another.

gamma ray Energy that comes from radioactive decay. Gamma rays are high-energy waves, as opposed to the alpha and beta rays, which are particles.

hadron One of the two primary types of particles, which have their own set of rules that describe their behavior and consist of either two or three quarks joined very closely together.

lepton One of the two primary classes of particles, which have a unique set of rules that describe their behavior, and they cannot be split into smaller particles.

matter The material that composes any object that has mass.

natural philosopher Someone who thinks about the natural world as opposed to the world of things that humans have built. The term "scientist" has largely replaced "natural philosopher."

neutron A neutral particle in the nucleus of every atom except for hydrogen. It is almost exactly the same size as the proton, and it consists of two down and one up quarks.

positron The antiparticle of the electron. It has the same mass as the electron, but the opposite charge.

positron emission tomography [PET] A medical imaging technique that detects the energy coming from the annihilation of an electron and a positron.

proton A positively charged particle that is in the nucleus of every atom. It is a hadron composed of two up quarks and one down quark.

quantum A small amount of some quantity, usually referring to energy. A quantum is the smallest possible step of energy.

quantum mechanics The theory that accurately describes the behavior of very small bits of matter or energy.

quark A particle discovered within the proton. There are six different types of quarks, each of which has a fraction of the charge of an electron or proton.

radioactive decay The emission of energy from an atom that triggers the atom's change from one form to another.

special relativity Albert Einstein's theory that says that nothing can travel faster than the speed of light. There are many other implications, including the existence of antimatter.

standard model The set of particles and forces that appears to describe all the observations made of matter.

theory A model of some aspect of the universe that accounts for observations and makes predictions about as yet unobserved phenomena.

FURTHER READING

Books

Ansdell, Megan. *The Big Bang Explained.* New York, NY: Enslow Publishing, 2018.

Borissov, Guennadi. *The Story of Antimatter: Matter's Vanished Twin.* Singapore: World Scientific Publishing, 2018.

Hilton, Lisa. *The Theory of Relativity*. New York, NY: Cavendish Square Publishing, 2016.

Lindsey, Michael. *Dark Matter, Antimatter, and Galaxies: Beyond the Standard Model.* New York, NY: Page Publishing, 2016.

Pamplona, Alberto Hernandez. *A Visual Guide to Energy and Movement.* New York, NY: Rosen Young Adult, 2017.

Rovelli, Carlo. *Seven Brief Lessons on Physics.* New York, NY: Riverhead Books, 2016.

Websites

CERN
home.cern
The European Organization for Nuclear Research discusses how it conducts experiments using instruments such as particle accelerators and detectors to study fundamental particles.

Institute of Physics
www.iop.org/resources/topic/archive/antimatter/index.html
The archive features articles on antimatter, particle detection, radioactivity, and other physics topics as well as video and audio files.

The Particle Adventure
www.particleadventure.org
This interactive website allows visitors to explore quarks, antimatter, extra dimensions, particle detectors, and more.

INDEX